rice & risotto

NEW HOLLAND

contents

introduction

Rice is the world's largest crop and is grown on every inhabited continent. Long grain rice, such as basmati rice from India and Pakistan, is great steamed and makes a fragrant bed for vegetables casseroles and curries. From Italy comes Arborio rice, which absorbs the beautiful flavours of the stock in which it's cooked to make risotto.

Brown rice has not had its husk removed and takes longer to cook. Many people, however, enjoy its nutty taste and make it part of a fibre-rich diet. Rice can be coked ahead of time and reheated, and leftovers can be transformed into tempting treats such as rice balls or fried rice. Store cooked rice by covering it with plastic wrap after it has cooled, and placing it in the refrigerator for up to three days.

An ancient Chinese proverb says 'without rice even the cleverest housewife cannot cook'. Today we might substitute the word 'chef' for 'housewife' but the rest of the sentence still rings true. Rice is one of the world's great staples – the original everyday food. White rice was once just a simple accompaniment to a meal or the occasional dessert, such as rice pudding, but rice consumption has changed significantly in recent decades as we embrace the culinary influences of Asian cuisine.

Today, consumers recognise rice as a versatile, healthy food that can complement the tastes of many international cuisines.

Europeans eat on average about 11 kilograms of rice per year. There are over 60,000 different varieties of rice grown throughout the world and there are many different ways of cooking it. Quick cooking rice is a recent innovation designed to help the time-poor chef.

NUTRITION
All varieties of rice are good for you. With the benefits of wholegrains, brown rice is the most nutritious rice variety but it takes longer to cook unless you use a quick-cooking variety. Brown rice has a bran layer which is removed in the milling process to create white varieties. It is a great source of niacin and magnesium (good for activating enzymes that contribute to energy production), a good source of iron and provides some protein and fibre. White rice contains about half the dietary fibre of brown. All rice is low in fat and salt, and is gluten free.

RICE AND THE GLYCAEMIC INDEX
Varieties range from low to high on the glycaemic index (low-GI foods are absorbed slower by the body which is believed to be healthier and better for weight management). Basmati, doongara and koshihikari (Japanese-style sushi rice) have a low GI value, as does brown rice. Arborio rice loses a lot of starch in the cooking process (such as risottos) which results in a high GI value.

STORING
Keep rice in a cool, dry place in an airtight container. Many brands now sell their rice products in resealable bags. If properly stored, white rice will last in your pantry for up to two years. While it doesn't actually go off, aged white rice will dry out and lose its flavour. The outer bran layer of brown rice contains oil which will eventually go rancid (and smell bitter) so use brown rice within 12 months.

COOKING

There are a few different ways of cooking rice, depending on what you're making and how much time you have. It's supposed to be easy but many will admit they can never get perfect fluffy rice. A rice cooker takes a lot of the guess work out of this task and there are many reasonably priced models available.

Probably the simplest method is boiling, but there are a few tricks to getting this right. One cup of raw rice makes about two cups when cooked. To boil, bring about eight cups of water to boiling point, then add the rice. Make sure you then turn the heat down to a gentle boil and let it cook uncovered for about 15 minutes for white rice and about 30 minutes for brown rice. Like pasta, you may need to check the rice is cooked through before removing from the heat and draining in a sieve. The truth is, boiled rice can be gluggy and unless you have perfected your technique, the way to lovely fluffy white rice is the absorption method. Follow the step-by-step instructions below.

HOW TO COOK PERFECT WHITE RICE

1. When measuring quantities keep in mind rice increases in volume, so one cup of raw rice produces two cups when cooked.

2. Place 1 cup of rice into a medium saucepan and add 2 cups of cold water. Make sure surface of rice is level to ensure it cooks evenly.

3. Bring to the boil, reduce heat and cook over medium-high for 8 minutes or until tunnels form in the rice and most of the water has been absorbed.

4. Turn off heat and cover with a tight-fitting lid for 10 minutes. This allows the rice to be steamed through and results in a fluffy texture.

5. Remove lid and run a fork through the rice to separate grains and avoid rice from setting into a solid mass.

RICE – A USER'S GUIDE

Basmati is an aromatic rice that is very popular. It is also a very long and firm grain. The grains of this drier rice stay separate so it's ideal for curries, tandoori, biryani, pilaf and other Indian and Middle Eastern dishes.

Medium grain is a soft, slightly clingy grain, although not as soft and clingy as short-grain varieties. It is one of the most popular all-purpose rice. Suitable for creamed rice, rice puddings, rice soups and casseroles.

Wild rice is not a rice at all. It is the seed of a special aquatic grass that is pre-cooked to shorten the cooking time to equal that of white rice. It's grown in North and South America.

Jasmine is commonly preferred in Asian cooking because of its delicate fragrance and soft texture. The slightly sticky but fluffy and separating rice is perfect in fried rice, stir-fries, Thai curries and other Asian dishes.

Brown rice has a nutty flavour and chewy texture because the nutritious bran layer has not been removed at milling. This is why it takes longer to cook than white rice. It's great in soups, casseroles, stuffings or as a healthier side dish with meals. Available in medium and long grain.

Japanese-style, or koshihikari as it's traditionally known, is basically sushi rice. It's a very short grain and quite sticky, so that it clumps together, which is especially good for sushi.

White long-grain rice is the most popular variety. It has a fluffy texture and the grains separate easily. Its neutral flavour makes it a great all-rounder with Asian-style dishes, rice salads and pilafs. Its neutral flavour goes well with everything.

Arborio rice was originally developed in northern Italy. This medium grain absorbs flavours. Its creamy texture makes it ideal for Italian risottos, paellas, soups, Greek dolmades, puddings and desserts.

The latest of the 'instant' rice varieties is microwave. The rice is pre-cooked in a special oven called a retort in a process that eliminates the potential for any bacteria to develop.It's similar to the canning process for vegetables, fruit or pre-cooked meals.

basic rice

Tomato rice

1. Combine the rice with tomato juice and beef stock in a saucepan. Bring to the boil, reduce heat to low, cover and cook for 15 minutes.

2. Season and remove pan from heat, drain and allow to stand covered for 10 minutes. Garnish with sliced scallions.

3. Great with steak and burgers.

1 cup medium-grain rice
1 cup tomato juice
1 cup beef stock
salt
4 scallions (green onions), sliced

Yellow rice

1. Combine the rice with turmeric and 4 cups water in a saucepan. Bring to the boil, reduce heat to low, cover and cook for 15 minutes.

2. Season and remove pan from heat, allow to stand covered for 10 minutes. Toss with lemon zest before serving.

2 cups medium-grain rice
1 teaspoon turmeric
salt
zest of ½ lemon, grated

Onion rice

1. Combine the rice with onion soup mix and 2 cups water in a saucepan. Bring to the boil, reduce heat to low, cover and cook for 15 minutes.

2. Season and remove pan from heat, allow to stand covered for 10 minutes. Top with onion rings to serve.

3. Great with steaks or any kind of chops.

1 cup medium-grain rice
½ packet onion soup mix
salt
fried onion rings

Orange rice

1. Combine the rice with orange juice and chicken stock in a saucepan. Bring to the boil, reduce heat to low, cover and cook for 15 minutes.

2. Season and remove pan from heat and allow to stand covered for 10 minutes.

3. This recipe is great served with chicken. You can also add nuts and sultanas to this recipe.

1 cup medium-grain rice
1 cup orange juice
1 cup chicken stock
salt

Apple rice

SERVES 4

1 cup medium-grain rice
1 cup apple juice
1 cup vegetable stock
salt
1 apple, chopped

1. Combine the rice with apple juice and vegetable oil in a saucepan. Bring to the boil, reduce heat to low, cover and cook for 15 minutes.

2. Season and remove pan from heat, and allow to stand covered for 10 minutes. Garnish with chopped apple.

3. Delicious with roast pork or pork chops.

Lemon rice

SERVES 4

1 cup medium-grain rice
¼ cup lemon juice
zest of ½ lemon
¼ teaspoon turmeric
salt

1. Combine the rice with the lemon juice, lemon zest, turmeric and ¼ cup water in a saucepan. Bring to the boil, reduce heat to low, cover and cook for 15 minutes.

2. Season and remove pan from heat, allow to stand covered for 10 minutes.

3. This rice is perfect with fish.

Fried rice

SERVES 6

6 dried mushrooms
4 tablespoons peanut oil
1 small clove garlic, crushed
⅛in (5mm) piece ginger,
  chopped
2 eggs, beaten with a little soy
  sauce
3oz (90g) cooked chicken or
  barbecued pork, diced
3oz (90g) shelled shrimp
  (prawns)
6 scallions (spring onions),
  chopped
6 cups cooked short-grain rice
salt
1 tablespoon soy sauce
1 tablespoon Chinese rice wine

1. Soak mushrooms in hot water for 20 minutes or until tender. Cut into small dice.
2. Heat half the oil with the garlic and ginger, then add eggs and fry without stirring until set and golden. Remove, cut omelette into small squares and reserve.
3. Heat remaining oil and fry mushrooms, chicken or pork, shrimp and scallions. Add rice and toss continuously with egg slice or fork until heated. Season with salt, then add reserved egg.
4. Combine soy sauce and wine, sprinkle over rice then toss again.

Spicy yoghurt rice

SERVES 4

1. Combine the rice with 1½ cups water in a saucepan. Bring to the boil, reduce heat to low, cover and cook for 15 minutes. Remove pan from heat, allow to stand covered for 10 minutes. Mix in yoghurt and salt while rice is hot.

2. Mix chillies and ginger through rice mixture.

3. Heat oil in a frying pan and carefully pop mustard seeds over a low heat. Add to rice with cilantro. Mix until combined, then serve.

4. This is a traditional Southern Indian rice dish served at room temperature as a curry accompaniment.

1 cup long-grain rice
1 cup natural yoghurt
1 teaspoon salt
2 green chillies, deseeded and thinly sliced
3in (8cm) piece fresh ginger, grated
1 tablespoon peanut oil
1 tablespoon black mustard seeds
¼ cup fresh cilantro (coriander), chopped

starters

Tuna, vegetable & rice fritters

SERVES 4

1. Combine all the ingredients.
2. Mix well and add enough water to create a batter.
3. Fry dessertspoons of the mixture in hot oil for approximately 3 minutes or until golden.
4. Serve with lemon wedges.

1 x 6oz (185g) can of tuna in olive oil
1 large onion, finely chopped
2 eggs
1 grated carrot
1 x 9oz (250g) packet of cooked wholegrain rice
½ cup of plain flour
salt and pepper to taste

Dolmades

MAKES 40

1. Mix the onion, rice, oil, herbs, salt and lemon juice in a bowl. Boil some water and soak the vine leaves in boiling water for 15 minutes.

2. Then place under cold water for 10 minutes, and then lie out on a tea towel to dry.

3. To wrap vine leaves: place one tablespoon of rice mixture in the centre of the leaf and wrap like a parcel. Use less mixture if the leaves are small.

4. Place the leaves in a saucepan and cover with boiling water. Add 1¾fl oz (50ml) of lemon juice to the water. Place a plate over the top of them and cook for an hour or until the vine leaves are cooked.

1 x 6oz (185g) can of tuna in olive oil
1 large onion, finely chopped
2 eggs
1 grated carrot
1 x 9oz (250g) packet cooked wholegrain rice
½ cup of plain flour
salt and pepper to taste

Pork lettuce rolls

SERVES 4

2 dried Chinese mushrooms
2 teaspoons vegetable oil
1 clove garlic, crushed
2in (5cm) piece fresh ginger,
  finely grated
4oz (125g) lean pork mince
4oz (125g) raw shrimp
  (prawns), shelled, deveined
  and finely chopped
4 scallions (spring onions),
  chopped
½ red bell pepper (capsicum),
  finely chopped
2oz (60g) canned bamboo
  shoots, drained and finely
  chopped
4 canned water chestnuts,
  drained and finely chopped
1 cup long-grain rice, cooked
  and kept warm
2 tablespoons dry sherry
1 tablespoon soy sauce
2 teaspoons hoisin sauce
1 round lettuce, leaves
  separated

1. Place mushrooms in a bowl, cover with boiling water and set aside to soak for 20 minutes or until mushrooms are tender. Drain, remove stalks if necessary and chop mushrooms finely.

2. Heat oil in a wok or frying pan over a medium heat, add garlic and ginger and stir-fry for 30 seconds. Add pork and stir-fry for 2–3 minutes or until pork is brown and cooked through.

3. Add shrimp, scallions, red bell pepper, bamboo shoots, water chestnuts and mushrooms to pan and stir-fry for 30 seconds or until shrimp change colour.

4. Add rice to prawn mixture and toss to combine. Stir in sherry, soy sauce and hoi sin sauce and cook, stirring, for 30 seconds or until mixture is heated.

5. Serve rice mixture and lettuce leaves separately and allow each person to place some of the rice mixture in a lettuce leaf. Roll up and eat with fingers.

Pork fried rice

SERVES 4

1 tablespoon olive oil
7oz (200g) marinated pork
　　fillet, diced
½ cup apple juice
2 cups vegetables such as,
　　carrots, wholegrain corn,
　　peas and beans
3 cups boiled rice
8 fresh lettuce leaves, whole,
　　depending on size of leaves
MARINADE
2 tablespoon soy sauce
1 clove garlic, crushed
2 tablespoons sweet chilli sauce

1. Mix together the marinade ingredients and marinate the pork for a few hours. Heat the oil in a large wok. Lightly stir-fry the diced pork until lightly golden brown. Add apple juice and simmer for 10–15 minutes. Remove meat from the wok.

2. Stir in all the vegetables, add the rice and stir-fry until rice is hot. Add the pork and mix well. Turn to very low heat and keep warm.

3. Twist each lettuce leaf into a cup and use a toothpick to hold it in place. Dish the fried rice into the lettuce cups and serve.

soup

Brown rice broth

1. Combine stock with vegetables and parsley in a large saucepan. Add bay leaf, tomato paste and rice. Season to taste. Cover and simmer for 1½ hours. Serve sprinkled with chopped parsley.

10 cups beef stock
4 carrots, chopped
1 onion, chopped
1 stalk celery, chopped
1 small turnip, chopped
3 whole sprigs parsley
1 bay leaf
1 tablespoon tomato paste
½ cup brown rice
¼ cup parsley, chopped

Curried rice soup

SERVES 4

1. Heat ghee or oil in a saucepan over a medium heat. Add onions and garlic and cook, stirring, for 2–3 minutes or until onions are golden. Stir in rice and curry powder and cook for 1 minute longer.

2. Add stock to pan and bring to the boil. Reduce heat to simmering and stir in cilantro. Cover and simmer for 12 minutes or until rice is tender.

3. Stir lemon juice into rice, top with yoghurt and serve immediately.

3 tablespoons ghee or vegetable oil
2 onions, thinly sliced
2 cloves garlic, crushed
½ cup long-grain rice
1 tablespoon curry powder
6 cups chicken stock
¼ cup fresh cilantro (coriander, chopped
2 tablespoons lemon juice
¼ cup natural yoghurt

Old-style chicken broth

SERVES 4

2lb 4oz (1kg) chicken pieces, breasts and thighs
1 lemon, sliced
1 teaspoon salt
freshly ground black pepper
1 bay leaf
3 tablespoons medium-grain rice
2 carrots, thinly sliced
1 stalk celery, sliced
2 leeks, washed thoroughly and sliced, or 2 white onions, thinly sliced
¼ cup parsley, chopped

1. Where possible, remove skin from chicken. Pour over 8 cups cold water with lemon slices and allow to soak half an hour.

2. Bring to boil, add salt, pepper and bay leaf, then simmer for 30 minutes, add rice and continue to cook an extra 40 minutes. When chicken is quite tender, remove from broth until tender.

3. Remove any skin from chicken and chop into small dice, replace in broth, check seasoning, cool and skim fat from broth. Reheat and serve sprinkled with parsley.

Shrimp soup

SERVES 4

17½oz (500g) raw shrimp
   (prawns), shelled and
   deveined, tails left intact
3 tablespoons fish sauce
2 tablespoons soy sauce
1 tablespoon lemon juice
½in (12mm) piece fresh ginger,
   finely grated
2 tablespoons vegetable oil
1 onion, sliced
1 clove garlic, crushed
2 tomatoes, peeled, deseeded
   and sliced
2 stalks celery, sliced
½ cup basmati or jasmine rice
8 cups fish stock or water
1oz (30g) bean sprouts
2 scallions (spring onions)
¼ cup fresh cilantro
   (coriander), chopped

1. Place shrimp, fish sauce, soy sauce, lemon juice and ginger in a bowl and toss to combine. Set aside to marinate for at least 15 minutes.

2. Heat oil in a saucepan over a medium heat, add onion and garlic and cook, stirring, for 2–3 minutes or until onion is tender and golden. Add tomatoes and celery and cook for 1 minute longer.

3. Add rice to onion mixture, then stir in stock or water and bring to the boil. Reduce heat and simmer for 10 minutes or until rice is almost tender.

4. Stir prawn mixture and bean sprouts into soup and simmer for 1–2 minutes or until shrimp change colour. Sprinkle with scallions and cilantro and serve immediately.

Spicy chicken soup

SERVES 4

1. Heat vegetable oil in a saucepan over a medium heat. Add onion, chillies and garlic and cook, stirring, for 2–3 minutes or until onion is tender. Stir in curry powder, ginger, shrimp paste, turmeric, cumin, nutmeg and black pepper to taste and cook, stirring, for 1 minute longer.

2. Add stock and rice to pan and bring to the boil. Reduce heat to simmering and simmer for 15 minutes. Stir chicken, cilantro and lemon juice into pan and simmer for 5 minutes longer or until chicken is cooked.

1 tablespoon vegetable oil
1 onion, finely chopped
2 fresh red chillies, chopped
1 clove garlic, crushed
1 tablespoon curry powder
½in (1cm) piece fresh ginger, finely grated
1 teaspoon dried shrimp paste
1 teaspoon ground turmeric
1 teaspoon ground cumin
½ teaspoon ground nutmeg
freshly ground black pepper
8 cups chicken stock
½ cup long-grain rice
9oz (250g) boneless chicken breast fillets, chopped
¼ cup, fresh cilantro (coriander), chopped
2 tablespoons lemon juice

Spicy pork soup

SERVES 4

1. Heat oil in a frying pan, add onion, garlic, chopped chilli, lemongrass and ginger and stir-fry for 2–3 minutes or until onion is golden. Add pork and stir-fry for 3–4 minutes.

2. Add rice to pork mixture and stir-fry for 1 minute. Stir in 8 cups of water with the fish sauce and lime or lemon juice and bring to the boil. Reduce and simmer for 15–20 minutes or until the rice is tender. Stir in scallions and cilantro. Sprinkle with sliced chilli and serve.

1 tablespoon vegetable oil
1 onion, sliced
2 cloves garlic, crushed
1 fresh red chilli, chopped, plus
  1 sliced
1 teaspoon chopped fresh
  lemongrass
½in (12mm) piece fresh ginger,
  chopped
9oz (250g) lean pork fillets,
  sliced
½ cup basmati rice
½ cup Thai fish sauce
2 tablespoons lime or lemon
  juice
4 scallions (spring onion),
  chopped
¼ cup fresh cilantro
  (coriander), chopped

Spinach and coconut soup

SERVES 4

1 tablespoon vegetable oil
1 onion, chopped
1 fresh red chilli, chopped
1 clove garlic, crushed
¼ teaspoon ground turmeric
2 cups water or fish stock
2 cups coconut milk
½ cup basmati or jasmine rice
2 tablespoons fish sauce
9oz (250g) firm white fish
  fillets, sliced
4oz (125g) raw shrimp
  (prawns), shelled and
  deveined
9oz (250g) shredded spinach
2 tablespoons shredded
  coconut, toasted

1. Heat oil in a saucepan over a medium heat, add onion, chilli and garlic and cook, stirring, for 2–3 minutes or until onion is golden and tender. Stir in turmeric.

2. Stir water or stock, coconut milk, rice and fish sauce into pan and bring to the boil. Reduce heat and simmer for 15 minutes. Add fish, shrimp and spinach and cook for 3–5 minutes longer or until shrimp just change colour. Sprinkle with coconut and serve immediately.

Rice soup

SERVES 4-6

1 tablespoon oil
3 cloves garlic, chopped
7oz (200g) lean pork, chopped
6 cups chicken stock
6 scallions (green onions),
    chopped
1 tablespoon fish sauce
⅔ cup long-grain rice
½ cup cilantro (coriander),
    chopped

1. Heat oil in a large saucepan, add garlic and pork and fry until pork is golden brown.
2. Simmer for 15–20 minutes or until soup is like thin porridge.
3. Serve soup immediately, sprinkled with chopped cilantro.

vegetarian

Mushroom & black olive risotto

SERVES 4

1. In a pan, gently simmer the stock. Cover the porcini with 7fl oz (200ml) boiling water, then leave to soak for 20 minutes. Drain and add the mushroom water to the stock. Heat the oil in a large heavy-based saucepan, add the onion and fresh mushrooms and sauté for 4–5 minutes. Add the rice and stir to coat with the oil, cooking for 1–2 minutes.

2. Add the porcini and the olives. Add one ladle of stock, simmer and stir until absorbed. Continue in this manner until all of the stock is used and the rice is just cooked.

3. Add the seasoning and the olive paste and cook for 2 minutes, uncovered, stirring constantly. Serve in bowls and use a potato peeler to shave the Parmesan over the risotto.

2 cups vegetable stock
1oz (30g) dried porcini
  mushrooms
3 tablespoons olive oil
1 onion, chopped
9oz (250g) large open
  mushrooms, chopped
1½ cup Arborio rice
2 tablespoons black olives,
  pitted and roughly chopped
salt and freshly ground black
  pepper
2 tablespoons black olive paste
fresh Parmesan to serve

Roasted pumpkin risotto

SERVES 4

1. Preheat the oven to 220°C (430°F).
2. Combine the pumpkin, 1 tablespoon olive oil, balsamic vinegar, salt and pepper in a non-stick baking tray. Bake in the oven for 20–25 minutes or until the pumpkin is golden.
3. Meanwhile, place the vegetable stock in a saucepan. Bring to a boil and simmer gently. Heat the remaining oil in a large saucepan over medium heat. Cook the onion and garlic for 2–3 minutes or until soft. Add the rice and stir until combined.
4. Add 1 cup of the stock and the rosemary leaves. Cook, stirring from time to time, until all the liquid is absorbed. Repeat this until all the stock is used and the rice is tender.
5. Stir in the pumpkin, goat's cheese, baby spinach and parsley and season to taste. Cook until heated through and the spinach has wilted. Serve immediately with crusty bread.

17½oz (500g) butternut pumpkin, peeled and cut into 2cm pieces
2 tablespoons olive oil
2 teaspoons balsamic vinegar
salt and freshly ground black pepper
5 cups vegetable stock
1 onion, finely chopped
3 cloves garlic, crushed
2 cups arborio rice
1 teaspoon dried rosemary leaves
4oz (125g) goat's cheese, crumbled
5oz (150g) baby spinach leaves, washed and trimmed
¼ cup fresh parsley, chopped

Risotto with spinach & gorgonzola

SERVES 6

4 cups vegetable stock
2 tablespoons olive oil
2 cloves garlic, crushed
1 onion, finely chopped
2 cups Arborio rice
½ cup white wine
5oz (150g) baby spinach
8oz (220g) Gorgonzola cheese,
    in small pieces
salt and freshly ground black
    pepper

1. Place stock in a saucepan and bring to the boil. Leave simmering.

2. Heat oil in a large saucepan, add garlic and onion, and cook for 5 minutes, or until soft. Add rice, and stir, until well coated.

3. Pour in wine, and cook, until the liquid has been absorbed. Add a ladle of the stock, stir continuously, until the liquid has been absorbed, then add the next ladle of stock. Keep adding stock this way, and stirring, until all the stock is used, and until the rice is cooked, but still a little firm to bite.

4. Add the spinach, cheese and seasonings. Stir and cook until spinach is just wilted and cheese has melted. Serve immediately.

Spinach risotto with almonds

SERVES 3

1 bunch English spinach
2 tablespoons oil
½ bunch scallions (green
    onions), chopped
⅔ cup Arborio rice
salt and freshly ground freshly
    ground black pepper
3 tablespoons lemon juice
3½oz (100g) seedless raisins
50g (2oz) almonds, blanched
    and toasted

1. Trim roots from the spinach just above the pink tip. Wash thoroughly, drain well and chop roughly.

2. Heat oil in a saucepan, add scallions and sauté a little. Add rice and stir until coated with oil and slightly coloured (about 30 seconds).

3. Add spinach, 1¾ cups hot water, salt, pepper and lemon juice. Cover and cook on medium heat for 10 minutes. Remove lid, stir to combine, add raisins, re-cover and cook for 5 minutes more. Turn off heat and stand covered for 5 minutes before serving. Sprinkle with almonds.

Lemon & broccoli risotto

SERVES 4

1. Place stock in a saucepan and simmer gently. Heat oil in a large heavy-based saucepan over a medium heat. Add onion and garlic. Cook, stirring, for 1–2 minutes or until onion is translucent.
2. Stir in rice. Cook for 1–2 minutes. Add wine. Cook, stirring, until liquid is absorbed. Add 1 ladle stock and cook, stirring occasionally until liquid is absorbed. Add another ladle of stock and cook as described above. Continue until all the stock is used and the rice is tender. Add broccoli 2–3 minutes before end of cooking time.
3. Stir in parsley, lemon zest and juice and freshly ground black pepper to taste. Remove pan from heat. Stand for 3 minutes then serve.

4 cups hot vegetable stock
1 tablespoon olive oil
1 onion, chopped
1 clove garlic, crushed
1½ cups Arborio rice
1 cup dry white wine
4oz (125g) broccoli florets
½ bunch fresh parsley, chopped
finely grated zest and juice of
    1 lemon
crushed black peppercorns

Asparagus & lemon risotto

1. In a pan, gently simmer the stock. Heat the oil in a large, heavy-based saucepan or frying pan, then add the onion and fry for 3–4 minutes, until golden. Add the rice and stir for 1 minute or until coated with the oil. Stir in the wine and bring to the boil, then reduce the heat and continue stirring for 4–5 minutes, until the wine has been absorbed by the rice.

2. Pour about one-third of the stock into the rice and simmer, stirring constantly for 4–5 minutes, until the stock has been absorbed. Add half the remaining stock and cook, stirring, until absorbed. Add the remaining stock and the asparagus and cook, stirring, for 5 minutes or until the rice and asparagus are tender but still firm to the bite.

3. Add the butter and half the Parmesan and season. Cook, stirring constantly, for 1 minute or until the butter and cheese have melted into the rice. Sprinkle with the remaining Parmesan, parsley and lemon zest.

2 tablespoons olive oil
1 onion, chopped
1½ cup Arborio rice
7fl oz (200ml) white wine
3 cups vegetable stock
3½oz (100g) asparagus tips, cut into bite-size pieces
2oz (60g) butter
2½oz (75g) Parmesan, grated
salt and freshly ground black pepper
2 tablespoons fresh parsley, chopped
finely grated zest of 1 lemon

Rice & apricot pilaf

SERVES 4

3 tablespoons oil or butter
1 large onion, finely chopped
1½ cups rice
3½ cups hot water
salt and freshly ground pepper
2 tablespoons parsley, finely
   chopped
2 tablespoons lemon juice
7oz (200g) dried apricots
2 tablespoons seedless raisins
2oz (60g) almonds, blanched
   and toasted

1. In a large saucepan heat oil or butter and fry the onion until pale golden in colour. Add the rice and stir 30 seconds to coat with oil.

2. Add the hot water, salt, pepper, parsley and lemon juice. Cover and simmer for 10 minutes.

3. Stir in the apricots (whole), raisins and almonds and simmer for 5 minutes more. Remove from heat and allow to stand, covered, for 5 minutes before serving.

Italian mushroom risotto

SERVES 4

3oz (90g) butter
1 onion, finely chopped
1 clove garlic, crushed
9oz (250g) mushrooms, sliced
2 cups Arborio rice
½ cup dry white wine
1 tablespoon tomato paste
1¼ cup vegetable stock, heated
Parmesan cheese

1. Place butter in frying pan, add onion and garlic and cook until onion is golden. Add mushrooms and cook over low heat for 2 minutes.

2. Add rice to the saucepan and cook over a medium heat, stirring constantly, for 3 minutes or until rice becomes translucent. Add wine and tomato paste, stirring until absorbed. Pour half a cup of hot stock into rice mixture and cook, stirring constantly, until liquid is absorbed. Continue cooking in this way until all the stock is used.

3. Remove from heat, add Parmesan and toss with fork to blend.

Risotto mould

1. Heat oil in a frying pan and sauté onions until golden. Add mushrooms and cook for 2–3 minutes or until tender.

2. Stir in rice and toss to combine with mixture. Pour in boiling stock a little at a time, stirring constantly until the rice is cooked and liquid is absorbed – about 15 minutes.

3. Preheat oven to 400°F/200°C. Fold butter, peas and Parmesan through the risotto and season to taste. Risotto should be slightly creamy. Spoon mixture into a suitable lightly greased ovenproof mould or bowl and bake or 10 minutes.

4. Turn out onto a platter or flat serving dish and serve.

¼ cup olive oil
2 onions, finely chopped
14oz (400g) mushrooms, sliced
2 cups quick-cooking brown rice
4 cups chicken stock, boiling
1oz (30g) butter
1½oz (45g) Parmesan cheese, grated
17½oz (500g) cooked fresh peas

Roasted vegetable risotto with pesto

SERVES 4

1. Preheat the oven to 460°F (240°C). Quarter the onion, remove the seeds from the bell peppers and cut the flesh into large chunks. Cut away tough stalks from asparagus and cut into lengths. Mix all these vegetables with 2 tablespoons of the olive oil and roast for 30 minutes, stirring once.

2. Meanwhile, begin the risotto. Heat the remaining olive oil and add the garlic and scallions. Add the rice and stir to coat. Add the white wine and stir until absorbed. Pour 1 cup of hot stock into rice mixture and cook, stirring constantly, until liquid is absorbed. Continue cooking in this way until all the stock is used.

3. When adding the last cup of stock, add the roasted vegetables and their juice and stir to combine. Add the Parmesan, sour cream and black pepper and serve immediately with a spoonful of pesto and some extra Parmesan crumbed on top.

1 large red onion
1 red bell pepper (capsicum)
1 yellow bell pepper (capsicum)
1 bunch asparagus
3 tablespoons olive oil
2 cloves garlic, finely chopped
4 scallions (spring onions), chopped
2 cups Arborio rice
¾ cup white wine
3½ cups vegetable stock, heated
2oz (60g) Parmesan cheese, grated
2 tablespoons sour cream
freshly ground black pepper
⅓ cup pesto

Risotto tricolore

SERVES 4

2 tablespoons olive oil
4 cloves garlic, finely chopped
2 red bell peppers (capsicums),
    cut into ⅛in (5mm) slices
2 yellow bell peppers
    (capsicums), cut into ⅛in
    (5mm) slices
2 green bell peppers
    (capsicums), cut into ⅛in
    (5mm) slices
2 cups Arborio rice
½ cup dry white wine
3½ cups vegetable stock, heated
1½oz (45g) butter
½ cup parsley, chopped
freshly ground black pepper

1. Heat the olive oil in a saucepan and cook the garlic gently. Add the bell peppers and continue cooking for 5 minutes. Add the rice and stir to coat. Add the wine and allow all the liquid to be absorbed.

2. Pour 1 cup hot stock into rice mixture and cook, stirring constantly, until liquid is absorbed. Continue cooking in this way until all the stock is used and the rice is tender.

3. Remove the risotto from the heat and add the butter, parsley and black pepper. Stir well and serve immediately.

Black beans & rice

SERVES 4

1 onion, chopped

1 green bell pepper (capsicum), chopped

2 cloves garlic, chopped

1½ teaspoons ground cumin

1 teaspoon dried thyme

½ teaspoon red pepper flakes

1 bay leaf

1 tablespoon olive oil

1 cup rice

14oz (400g) canned diced tomatoes

1 green chilli, chopped

14oz (400g) canned black beans

1 tablespoon apple cider vinegar

½ teaspoon salt

½ teaspoon freshly ground black pepper

1. Sauté onion, bell pepper, garlic, cumin, thyme, red pepper flakes, bay leaf and olive oil until onion is tender, about 5 minutes.

2. Stir in rice, tomatoes, chilli, black beans, vinegar, salt, and pepper and 2 cups water.

3. Bring to boil. Reduce heat and simmer, covered, until rice is tender, about 20 minutes. Let stand for 5 minutes before serving.

Lentil & rice pilaf

SERVES 4

1. Bring a large saucepan of water to the boil. Add rice and lentils, reduce heat and simmer for 15 minutes or until they're tender. Drain and set aside.

2. Heat 2 teaspoons oil in a frying pan over a medium heat, add garam masala, cumin and cilantro and cook, stirring, for 2 minutes. Add rice and lentil mixture and cook, stirring, for 4 minutes longer. Remove from heat, set aside and keep warm.

3. Heat remaining oil in a separate frying pan over a medium heat, add onions and cook, stirring, for 6 minutes or until onions are soft and golden. Sprinkle onions over pilaf. Serve hot, warm or at room temperature.

1 cup long-grain rice
7oz (200g) green lentils
3 tablespoons vegetable oil
2 teaspoons garam masala
1 teaspoon ground cumin
1 teaspoon ground coriander
3 onions, sliced

Rice with onion & cilantro

SERVES 4-6

1. Cook rice in coconut cream and 2 cups water for 20 minutes or until tender and liquid has been absorbed. Stir in salt.
2. Heat oil in a wok or heavy-based frying pan and stir-fry onion, garlic and ginger for 3 minutes.
3. Add chilli, poppy seeds, cashew nuts, cloves, cinnamon and curry powder and stir-fry for about 30 seconds or until spices smell fragrant.
4. Add rice to spice mixture and cook until heated through.
5. Add the scallions and cilantro to the mixture just before serving.

2 cups long-grain rice
3½ cups coconut cream
1 teaspoon salt
1 onion, finely chopped
1 clove garlic, chopped
2 tablespoons peanut oil
3in (75mm) piece fresh ginger, finely chopped
1 teaspoon ground chilli
2 tablespoons poppy seeds
1 cup cashew nuts
6 whole cloves
1 teaspoon ground cinnamon
2 teaspoons curry powder
2 scallions (spring onions), finely sliced
¼ cup fresh cilantro (coriander)

Savoury tomato & olive rice bake

SERVES 4

1 cup long-grain rice
1 onion, finely chopped
1 carrot, washed and cut into
 ½in (1cm) cubes
2 stalks celery, sliced
½ cup pitted olives
1 chicken stock cube
2½ cups tomato pasta sauce

1. Preheat oven to 350°F (180ºC). Place rice in a medium casserole dish and sprinkle onion, carrot, celery and olives over the rice.
2. Crumble the stock cube into the tomato pasta sauce and pour over the rice mixture.
3. Cover and cook for 45 minutes, or until rice is tender.

Malay vegetable salad

SERVES 4

2 tablespoons vegetable oil
4oz (125g) tofu, cubed
1 sweet potato, thinly sliced
1 cup brown rice, cooked and
  cooled
9oz (250g) bean sprouts
15oz (440g) fresh pineapple,
  diced
4oz (125g) snowpeas
8 scallions (spring onions),
  sliced
2 cucumbers, sliced
½ cup fresh basil leaves
1 fresh red chilli, sliced
2 tablespoons chopped peanuts
LIME AND CHILLI DRESSING
¼ cup lime juice
2 tablespoons soy sauce
2 tablespoons chilli sauce
1 fresh red chilli, chopped
1 clove garlic, crushed
½ teaspoon brown sugar
½ teaspoon dried shrimp paste

1. Heat oil in a frying pan over a medium heat, add tofu and cook, turning frequently, for 3–4 minutes, or until golden. Drain on absorbent paper.

2. Add sweet potato to same pan and cook, turning frequently, for 3–4 minutes or until golden. Drain on absorbent paper.

3. Arrange rice, bean sprouts, pineapple, snowpeas, scallions (spring onions), cucumbers, tofu, sweet potato, basil and sliced chilli attractively on a serving platter.

4. To make dressing, combine lime juice, soy sauce, chilli sauce, chopped chilli, garlic, sugar and shrimp paste. Drizzle dressing over salad, sprinkle with peanuts and serve.

seafood

Saffron & surf clam risotto

SERVES 4

1. On medium heat put the virgin olive oil, onion and garlic in a large pot and cook for 1 minute with a lid.
2. Add the rice and stir with a wooden spatula.
3. Add the white wine, saffron and cook slowly until the rice starts becoming dry (around 5 minutes).
4. Add the chicken stock, seasoning, mixed herbs,
5. pipies and surf clams and cook until all the shells have opened and the rice is cooked (around 15 minutes). Keep stirring frequently to avoid the rice sticking to the pot.
6. Serve with salad and crispy ciabatta bread.

115ml (4fl oz) virgin olive oil
1 onion, finely sliced
4 cloves garlic, finely chopped
14oz (400g) arborio rice
370ml (130z) dry white wine
pinch of saffron
2 cups chicken stock
salt and pepper
1 tablespoon mixed fresh
    herbs, chopped
510g (18oz) pipies
510g (18oz) surf clams

Seafood paella

SERVES 4

1. Heat 1 tablespoon of oil in a large frying pan or wok and cook shrimp and squid over a high heat for 1 minute. Remove from pan and set aside. Add remaining oil and cook onion, garlic, ginger and chilli for 4–5 minutes.

2. Bring 1 cup of water to boil. Add saffron and infuse for 3 minutes. Add chicken to the pan and cook for 2 minutes. Add rice and mix to combine completely with other ingredients. Add saffron mixture and 1 cup of stock. Stir, bring to the boil and reduce heat. Simmer, stirring occasionally, for 10 minutes, or until liquid is absorbed. Add remaining stock and simmer, stirring occasionally, for 10 minutes longer, or until liquid is almost absorbed.

3. Add mussels and peas, cover and cook over low heat for 5 minutes. Discard any mussels that do not open, stir in the scallops, cilantro, lemon zest and reserved shrimp and squid. Cover and cook for 5 minutes longer. Serve immediately.

2 tablespoons olive oil
14oz (400g) raw shrimp (prawns), shelled and deveined
2½oz (75g) squid tubes, cut in rings
½ red onion, sliced
1 clove garlic, crushed
2in (5cm) piece fresh ginger, grated
1 small red chilli, finely chopped
9oz (250g) chicken fillets, finely sliced
¼ teaspoon saffron threads
1½ cups long-grain rice
2 cups chicken stock
5oz (150g) mussels
3½oz (100g) fresh peas
3½oz (100g) fresh scallops
¼ cup fresh cilantro (coriander)
finely grated zest of ½ lemon
salt and freshly ground black pepper

Butterflied shrimp in lemon sauce

SERVES 4

17½oz (500g) raw king shrimp
  (prawns)
2 cups medium-grain rice
2 tablespoons olive oil
1 red bell pepper (capsicum),
  sliced
1 green bell pepper (capsicum),
  sliced
1 small onion, sliced
1 medium carrot, diced
juice of 1 lemon
2 scallions (spring onions),
  finely chopped
MARINADE
2 teaspoons sherry
1 teaspoon soy sauce
1 egg white
½in (1cm) piece ginger, grated
1 teaspoon cornflour
zest of 2 lemons

1. Remove shells from shrimp but leave tails intact. Using a small knife, remove vein from back, rinse and pat dry. Blend marinade ingredients, add shrimp and marinate for 20 minutes.

2. Combine the rice with 3 cups water in a saucepan. Bring to the boil, reduce heat to low, cover and cook for 15 minutes. Remove pan from heat, allow to stand covered for 10 minutes.

3. Meanwhile, heat oil in wok or saucepan and stir-fry the vegetables for 5 minutes. Remove from pan, add the shrimp and fry, stirring constantly, until just turning pink, about 3–4 minutes. Return vegetables to the wok, add lemon juice. Serve shrimp and vegetables on rice, garnished with scallions.

Nasi goreng

SERVES 6

2 cups long-grain rice, rinsed
1½ tablespoons peanut oil
2 eggs, lightly beaten
4 scallions (green onions),
    finely sliced
2 cloves garlic, crushed
2 small red chillies, deseeded
    and finely chopped
10½oz (300g) chicken thigh
    fillets, diced
1 carrot, finely sliced or grated
2 cups shredded bok choy
3½oz (100g) shrimp (prawns),
    peeled and cooked
2–3 tablespoons kecap manis
1 tablespoon soy sauce

1. Cook rice in boiling salted water for 10–12 minutes or until cooked. Drain and rinse.

2. Heat 2 teaspoons oil in a wok. Add egg and swirl to coat the wok to form an omelette. Turn omelette and cook the other side. Remove and cut into thin strips.

3. Heat remaining oil in wok. Add scallions, garlic and chilli and cook for 1–2 minutes. Add chicken and stir-fry for 3 minutes. Add carrot, bok choy, shrimp, kecap manis and soy sauce and stir-fry until bok choy wilts.

4. Add rice to mixture and stir-fry until heated through. Serve rice with strips of omelette, fried scallions and the sambal of your choice.

Leek and shrimp risotto

SERVES 4

1. Melt butter in a saucepan over a low heat, add leeks and cook, stirring occasionally, until leeks are soft, golden and caramelised. Add shrimp and cook, stirring, for 3 minutes or until they just change colour. Remove prawn mixture from pan and set aside.

2. Add rice to pan and cook over a medium heat, stirring, for 4 minutes. Stir in ⅔ cup hot stock and ¼ cup wine and cook, stirring constantly, over a medium heat until liquid is absorbed. Continue cooking in this way until all the stock and wine are used and the rice is tender.

3. Return prawn mixture to pan and add green peppercorns. Mix gently to combine and cook for 3 minutes longer or until heated through.

1oz (30g) butter
4 leeks, sliced and washed
17½oz (500g) medium raw shrimp (prawns), shelled and deveined
2½ cups Arborio rice
4 cups fish stock, heated
1 cup dry white wine
1 tablespoon canned green peppercorns, drained

Mussel risotto

SERVES 4

1. Place oil in a saucepan over medium heat. Add onion, garlic and bell pepper and cook for 2 minutes.
2. Add rice and half the wine, stirring constantly until liquid is absorbed. Add mussels and the other half of the wine.
3. Add herbs, cover and cook until rice and mussels are cooked, stirring frequently. Discard any mussels that do not open. Serve sprinkled with grated Parmesan.

2 tablespoons olive oil
1 onion, finely chopped
2 cloves garlic, finely chopped
1 red bell pepper (capsicum), diced
1½ cups Arborio rice
2½ cups dry white wine
2lb 4oz (1kg) mussels, cleaned
1 sprig rosemary, leaves removed and chopped
2 sprigs thyme, leaves removed and stalks discarded
1½oz (45g) Parmesan cheese, grated

Pacific curry with lemon rice

SERVES 4

3 tablespoons peanut oil
½in (12mm) piece ginger,
  finely chopped
1 clove garlic, crushed
17½oz (500g) raw shrimp
  (prawns), shelled and
  deveined
2 onions, sliced, or 6 French
  shallots, sliced
1 tablespoon curry powder
1½ cups coconut milk or
  chicken stock
1 green cucumber, halved
  lengthwise, deseeded, then
  cut in thick slices
2 teaspoons lemon juice
1 teaspoon sugar
salt
3 teaspoons cornflour
  dissolved in little water
LEMON RICE
1 cup medium-grain rice
¼ cup lemon juice
zest of ½ lemon zest
¼ teaspoon turmeric

1. Heat oil in wok or frying pan. Add garlic and ginger – when they change colour, discard. Add shrimp to the flavoured oil, fry until they turn pink, remove and reserve. Add more oil if needed and cook onions for 2 minutes, add curry powder and stir-fry for 1 minute. Blend in coconut milk and heat until boiling, add cucumber and simmer for a few minutes. Add lemon juice, sugar and salt to taste, replace shrimp, add cornflour and stir until it boils and thickens.

2. To make the rice, bring 1¾ cups water, lemon juice, grated lemon zest and turmeric to the boil. Add the rice, cover and cook for 15 minutes. Remove from heat, and allow to stand covered for 10 minutes. Salt to taste and garnish with scallions. Serve with the shrimp.

Shrimp with basil and rice

SERVES 4-6

2 tablespoons oil
1 egg, lightly beaten
1 onion, chopped
2 cloves garlic, chopped
2 teaspoons shrimp paste
1 large tomato, chopped
2 scallions (green onions),
    sliced
2 tablespoons oyster sauce
5 cups cooked long-grain rice
15 fresh basil leaves
13oz (375g) cooked school
    shrimp (prawns), peeled

1. Heat 1 tablespoon of the oil in a large frying pan. Add beaten egg and cook 1–2 minutes each side, remove from pan and cut into thin strips.

2. Heat remaining 1 tablespoon oil in pan, add onion and garlic and fry for 2 minutes. Stir in shrimp paste, mixing well.

3. Add all remaining ingredients and cook for 2–3 minutes, stirring occasionally. Serve topped with the sliced egg.

Saffron rice with seafood

SERVES 4

1. Heat the saffron in the stock and leave to infuse. Heat the olive oil in a frying pan, paella or flattish casserole dish and gently cook the onions until soft and golden. Add the rice and cook, stirring until well coated with oil. Add the hot stock, stirring until mixture comes to the boil, then reduce the heat and simmer gently for 10 minutes.

2. Add the shrimp and scallops, pressing gently into the rice. Continue to cook for 5 minutes. Add the mussels or clams, which should open with the heat. If you have a lid, partly cover the rice. When the rice is tender (about 18–20 minutes) remove from the heat and gently fluff up the rice with a fork. Sprinkle cilantro over and serve.

good pinch of saffron
3 cups fish or chicken stock
2 tablespoons olive oil
2 onions, chopped
1¼ cups long-grain rice, rinsed
9oz (250g) raw shrimp
  (prawns), shelled and
  deveined
9oz (250g) scallops
12 mussels or baby clams,
  cleaned
small bunch cilantro
  (coriander)

Salmon cutlets with salsa & wild rice

SERVES 6

1. Preheat oven to 350°F (180°C). Bone cutlets and lightly grease both sides with melted butter, then place in the oven for 10–15 minutes.

2. To make the salsa, mix all ingredients in a serving bowl.

3. Combine the rice with 4½ cups water in a saucepan. Bring to the boil, reduce heat to low, cover and cook for 30 minutes. Remove pan from heat, allow to stand covered for 10 minutes.

4. Serve cutlets on a bed of salad greens with salsa and rice.

6 fresh salmon cutlets
2oz (60g) butter, melted
3 cups brown and wild rice
  blend
SALSA
1 small red onion, finely
  chopped
2 red bell peppers (capsicums),
  roasted, peeled and finely
  chopped
2 tablespoons sun-dried
  tomatoes, finely chopped
½ cup basil leaves, finely
  chopped
8 black olives, stoned and
  chopped
½ teaspoon lemon juice
½ teaspoon oil from sun-dried
  tomatoes jar
salt and freshly ground black
  pepper

Seafood & broccoli risotto

SERVES 4

1 tablespoon sunflower oil
6 French eschalots, chopped
1 clove garlic, finely chopped
1 red or yellow bell pepper
(capsicum), deseeded and
diced
9oz (250g) long-grain brown
rice
2 cups vegetable stock
9oz (250g) chestnut
mushrooms, sliced
1 cup dry white wine
14oz (400g) marinara mix
9oz (250g) broccoli, cut into
small florets
¼ cup fresh flat-leaf parsley,
chopped
freshly ground black pepper

1. Heat the oil in a large saucepan, add the eschalots, garlic and bell pepper and cook for 5 minutes or until softened, stirring occasionally. Add the rice and cook for 1 minute, stirring, until well coated in the oil.
2. In a separate pan, bring the stock to the boil. Add the mushrooms, wine and 5fl oz (150ml) of the stock to the rice mixture. Bring to the boil, stirring, then simmer, uncovered, for 15 minutes or until most of the liquid is absorbed, stirring often. Add another 7fl oz (200ml) of stock and cook for 15 minutes or until it is absorbed, stirring frequently.
3. Add the seafood and most of the remaining stock and stir frequently for 5 minutes or until the rice is cooked but firm to the bite. Add the rest of the stock, if necessary, and make sure the seafood is cooked through. Meanwhile, cook the broccoli in boiling water for 3 minutes or until tender. Drain well, stir into the risotto with the parsley and season with black pepper.
4. The secret to cooking a good risotto is to keep adding just enough liquid and to stir as much as possible. You can use any mixture in this recipe of seafood.

Wild rice & dill fish

SERVES 6

6 fish fillets (for example, ocean perch, bream or snapper)

1½ cups cooked brown rice and wild rice blend

7oz (200g) canned crab meat, drained

¼ cup finely chopped scallions (shallots)

1 tomato, peeled, deseeded and chopped

½ cup fresh dill, chopped

1 egg, separated

freshly ground black pepper

½ cup white wine

1 cucumber, peeled and deseeded

½oz (15g) butter

1 tablespoon plain flour

½ cup cream

1. Skin fish fillets if necessary. Preheat the oven to 350°F (180°C).

2. Combine wild rice, crab meat, shallots, tomato, half the dill, the egg white and pepper.

3. Roll each fillet into a circle and secure the ends together with a toothpick. Place in a casserole dish and fill the centre of each roll with rice mixture. Pour over the white wine, cover with foil and bake for 40–45 minutes until cooked through. Lift each fillet onto a serving plate and keep warm. Strain the liquid and use to make the sauce.

4. Cut the cucumber into thin slices. Pan-fry in butter until just tender. Set aside. Blend the flour with the liquid from the fish. Add the cream, the egg yolk and the remaining dill and bring to the boil. Serve with the fish rolls and garnish with braised cucumber.

Scallop & tomato risotto

SERVES 4

1.   Preheat a medium saucepan over medium-low heat. Add the rice and cook, stirring, for 1 minute. Reduce the heat to low, add ½ cup hot stock and cook, stirring constantly, until liquid is absorbed. Continue cooking in this way until all the stock is used and the rice is creamy and tender.

2.   Heat a large non-stick frying pan on medium-high heat. Cook the scallops for 1 minute on each side, then transfer to a medium bowl.

3.   Add the tomatoes and scallops to the risotto and stir through to warm and combine.

14oz (400g) Arborio rice
4½ cups fish stock, heated
20 scallops, roe removed
8 Roma tomatoes, diced

Tuna crumble

SERVES 4

1. Preheat oven to 380°F (190°C). Combine the rice with 1½ cups water in a saucepan. Bring to the boil, reduce heat to low, cover and cook for 15 minutes. Remove pan from heat, allow to stand covered for 10 minutes.

2. To make topping, mix breadcrumbs, oats, cheese and basil together until well combined.

3. In an ovenproof dish mix rice, tomatoes, tuna and capers. Sprinkle topping over and bake for 20 minutes or until topping is golden.

1 cup cooked long-grain rice
28oz (800g) chopped tomatoes
15oz (425g) canned tuna in water
2 tablespoons capers, drained
TOPPING
½ cup toasted breadcrumbs
½ cup rolled oats
3oz (90g) aged Cheddar, grated
1 teaspoon dried basil

Seafood & vegetable salad

SERVES 6

2 cups long-grain rice, cooked and cooled
9oz (250g) cooked shrimp (prawns), shelled and deveined
9oz (250g) canned crab meat, drained and flaked
4oz (125g) boneless white fish fillet or raw tuna, thinly sliced (optional)
3oz (90g) button mushrooms, sliced
6 scallions (spring onions), sliced
1 carrot, thinly sliced
1oz (30g) green beans, sliced
1 egg omelette, thinly sliced
RICE VINEGAR DRESSING
½ cup rice vinegar
2 tablespoons mirin or dry sherry
1 tablespoon soy sauce
1 tablespoon sugar

1. Place rice, shrimp, crab meat, fish (if using), mushrooms, scallions, carrot and beans in a large salad bowl and toss to combine.

2. To make dressing, place vinegar, mirin or sherry, soy sauce and sugar in a bowl and whisk to combine. Drizzle dressing over salad, cover and refrigerate, stirring occasionally, for 4–6 hours. Just prior to serving, top with omelette strips.

meat

Beef & sprout salad

SERVES 4

1. Heat oil in a wok or frying pan over a medium heat, add beef and stir-fry for 2–3 minutes or until beef is brown. Remove beef from pan and place in a bowl.

2. Add onion, lemongrass and garlic to pan and stir-fry for 2–3 minutes or until onion is golden. Add onion mixture, fish sauce and lemon juice to beef, toss to combine and set aside.

3. Place rice, bean sprouts, scallions, tomatoes, carrot and mint in a bowl and toss to combine. Line a serving platter with rice mixture, then top with beef mixture and sprinkle with cashew nuts.

1 tablespoon vegetable oil
9oz (250g) fillet steak, thinly sliced
1 onion, sliced
1 stalk fresh lemongrass, chopped
1 clove garlic, crushed
2 tablespoons fish sauce
1 tablespoon lemon juice
2 cups long-grain rice, cooked and cooled
2oz (60g) bean spouts
8 scallions (spring onions), sliced
2 tomatoes, chopped
1 carrot, thinly sliced
¼ cup fresh mint, chopped
2oz (60g) roasted cashew nuts

Beef keema

SERVES 4

1. Heat oil in a frying pan over a medium heat. Add onions, garlic and ginger and cook, stirring, for 3–4 minutes or until onions are golden and tender. Add beef and cook, stirring, for 5 minutes or until beef is well browned.

2. Stir cilantro, chilli and yoghurt into beef mixture and cook for 1 minute. Remove pan from heat.

3. Place rice, stock, cloves and cinnamon stick in a large saucepan and bring to the boil over a medium heat. Reduce heat to simmering, cover and simmer for 45 minutes. Remove pan from heat and stand, covered, for 5 minutes.

4. Lightly fork onion and beef mixture through rice and heat over a low heat, stirring, for 4–5 minutes, until keema is heated through

3 tablespoons vegetable oil
2 onions, sliced
1 clove garlic, crushed
½in (12mm) piece fresh ginger, finely grated
17½oz (500g) lean beef mince
¼ cup fresh cilantro (coriander), chopped
1 fresh red chilli, chopped
¼ cup natural yoghurt
2 cups brown rice
4 cup beef stock
2 whole cloves
1 cinnamon stick

Lamb fillets with salsa pilaf

SERVES 4

2 lamb fillets, about 24oz (750g)
1 clove garlic, crushed
1 tablespoon lemon juice
2 teaspoons olive oil
salt and freshly ground black pepper
1 cup medium-grain rice
2oz (60g) pine nuts, roasted
2 tablespoons currants
10½oz (300g) tomato salsa

1. Trim the lamb fillets. Place in a dish and add garlic, lemon juice, oil, salt and pepper. Cover and stand for 30 minutes.

2. Combine the rice with 1½ cups water in a saucepan. Bring to the boil, reduce heat to low, cover and cook for 15 minutes. Remove from heat and allow to stand covered for 10 minutes. Heat a small saucepan, add pine nuts and shake over heat until they colour. Add the currants and pine nuts to the rice, mix well and set aside.

3. Heat the barbecue grill plate and oil lightly. Place lamb on grill and cook for 6–8 minutes, turning to cook on all sides, (cook longer for well done). Rest the lamb for 5 minutes before slicing into ½in (12mm) slices. Heat the salsa in a small saucepan.

4. Using a cup or mould, form a mound of rice on the plate. Pour salsa over the rice and arrange lamb slices on the plate.

Lamb with spiced rice

SERVES 6-8

24oz (750g) lean lamb, finely chopped
2oz (60g) butter
2 teaspoons salt
½ teaspoon black pepper
½ teaspoon allspice
½ teaspoon ground nutmeg
¼ teaspoon ground cinnamon
¼ teaspoon ground saffron
2 cups basmati rice
3½ cups chicken stock, boiling
½ cup pine nuts

1. Lightly brown meat in butter. Add salt and spices and stir for 2 minutes.

2. Add the rice, stir and add the boiling chicken stock and mix well. Bring back to the boil.

3. Cover and simmer for 20–25 minutes or until rice is tender and stock is absorbed.

4. Let cool for 30 minutes and put in large serving dish, ready to serve. Serve with natural yoghurt if desired.

5. While the rice is cooling sauté ½ cup pine nuts in 3–4 tablespoons olive oil until light brown. Garnish rice and meat with the sautéed pine nuts and serve.

Bacon & pea risotto

SERVES 4

1. In a large saucepan, sauté bacon and onion for about 5 minutes or until onion is soft.
2. Add rice and sage and stir to coat rice in bacon and onion mixture.
3. Pour 1 cup of hot stock into rice mixture and cook, stirring constantly, until liquid is absorbed. Repeat with another cup of stock.
4. Continue adding stock 1 cup at a time until the rice is tender and all the liquid has been absorbed. With the last addition of stock, add the peas.
5. When all the stock is absorbed, season risotto with pepper and ladle into bowls. Top with Parmesan and serve immediately.

3 rashers rindless bacon, cut into thin strips
1 onion, finely chopped
1½ cup Arborio rice
1 teaspoon dried sage
5 cups chicken stock, heated
2 cups frozen peas
freshly ground black pepper
1½oz (45g) Parmesan cheese

Stir-fried pork & vegetables

SERVES 4

1. Heat oil in a wok or frying pan over a medium heat, add ginger and stir-fry for 30 seconds. Add pork and stir-fry for 2–3 minutes or until just cooked.

2. Add eggplant, green bell peppers and scallions to pan and stir-fry for 2–3 minutes or until vegetables are just tender.

3. Stir miso, sake or sherry, soy sauce and sugar into pan and stir-fry for 30 seconds. Stir in cornflour mixture and cook, stirring, for 1–2 minutes or until mixture boils and thickens. Reduce heat and simmer for 1–2 minutes longer.

4. Divide hot rice between serving bowls, top with vegetable mixture and serve immediately.

2 tablespoons vegetable oil
½in (12mm) piece fresh ginger, grated
4oz (125g) lean pork mince
4 baby eggplants, cut into 2in (5cm) lengths
2 green bell peppers (capsicums), chopped
2 scallions (spring onions), sliced
2 tablespoons miso paste
1 tablespoon sake or dry sherry
1 tablespoon soy sauce
1 tablespoon sugar
1 teaspoon cornflour, blended with 2 teaspoons water
2 cups brown rice, cooked and kept warm

Surf & turf risotto

SERVES 4

2 onions, sliced
⅓ cup olive oil
4 cloves garlic, chopped
14oz (400g) eye fillet, cut into
    2 pieces
10 scallions (spring onions),
    chopped
1 red bell pepper (capsicum),
    sliced into strips
2 cups Arborio rice
½ cup dry white wine
4 cups chicken stock, heated
2 lobster tails, cooked and
    chopped
1½oz (45g) Parmesan cheese,
    grated
½ cup parsley, chopped
1 tablespoon sour cream

1. Preheat the oven to 430°F (220°C).
Toss the onions with half the oil and bake
for 30–40 minutes, tossing frequently, until
golden. Set aside until the risotto is finished
and ready to serve.

2. Meanwhile, heat the remaining olive oil
and gently fry the garlic for 1–2 minutes.
Add the beef and sauté over a high heat
until seared and crisp on both sides.
Remove from the pan and keep warm,
wrapped in foil.

3. Add the scallions and bell pepper to the
garlic and sauté until softened.

4. Add the rice and stir to coat, then add
the wine and simmer, stirring, until the liquid
is absorbed. Pour 1 cup hot stock into rice
mixture and cook, stirring constantly, until
liquid is absorbed. Continue cooking in this
way until all the stock has been added. With
the last addition of stock, add the lobster
meat and stir. When almost all of the liquid
has been absorbed and the rice is tender,
stir through the Parmesan, parsley and sour
cream.

5. Meanwhile, remove the warm meat
from the foil and slice thinly. Serve the
risotto in individual bowls, fan out the meat
and place on top of the risotto. Garnish with
the onions and serve immediately.

Lemon veal & vegetable rice

SERVES 4

7oz (200g) lean veal strips
⅔oz (20g) butter
⅓fl oz (10ml) olive oil
juice of one lemon
½ cup finely chopped parsley
salt and pepper to taste
1 bunch asparagus, freshly
   chopped
½ sliced red bell pepper
   (capsicum)
1 onion, finely chopped
1 tablespoon water
9oz (250g) cooked long grain
   rice

1. Cook veal strips in $^1/_3$oz (10g) of butter and olive oil over medium heat for 3 minutes.

2. Add the lemon juice and parsley, salt and pepper.

In a small container, combine asparagus, bell pepper and onion with a tablespoon of water and a $^1/_3$oz 10g of butter.

3. Add salt and pepper to taste.

4. Cover and cook on high for 2 minutes then stir the vegetable mixture through long grain rice. Serve to accompany the lemon veal.

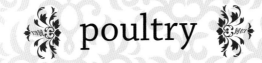

poultry

Fried rice with chicken & vegetables

SERVES 2

1. Place the sauces, sugar and pepper into a small bowl and have all other ingredients ready to use.

2. Heat the wok over high heat and add oil. Add the garlic and fry for 5 seconds before adding the chicken. Stir-fry over high heat until the chicken turns white.

3. Crack in the egg and move it gently around the wok for a few seconds before mixing it with the chicken.

4. Add the rice and stir-fry for 30 seconds (if using cold rice, stir-fry for 2–3 minutes until hot). Then add the cabbage, carrot, onion and tomato and cook for 1 minute.

5. Add the combined sauces, sugar and pepper and stir-fry until well combined.

6. Add the garlic chives, turn off the heat, mix through and serve.

2 teaspoons oyster sauce
1 teaspoon light soy sauce
½ teaspoon Thai seasoning sauce
1 teaspoon sugar
¼ teaspoon white pepper
1 teaspoon vegetable oil
¼ teaspoon garlic, minced
3½oz (100g) chicken thigh or breast fillet, thinly sliced
1 egg
2 cups cooked rice, hot or cold
½ cup white cabbage, shredded
¼ cup carrot, julienned
¼ cup onion, thinly sliced lenghtways
1 small or ½ large tomatoe, sliced into thin wedges
¼–½ cup garlic chives, cut into ¾in (2cm) lenghts

Casablanca chicken & yellow rice

SERVES 6

1. Fry chicken pieces in butter and oil until golden, then remove. Fry onions, garlic and spices. Replace chicken, toss in spice onion mixture. Add apricot nectar, wine, salt and pepper.

2. Cover, cook over moderate heat for 30–40 minutes or until tender. During last 10 minutes add prunes, apricots, honey and lemon juice. Check seasoning. Serve on bed of yellow rice (see recipe). Garnish with extra fruit and sprinkle with sesame seeds.

3lb 5oz (1½kg) chicken pieces
1oz (30g) butter
2 tablespoons oil
2 large onions, thinly sliced
1 clove garlic, crushed
2in (5cm) piece fresh ginger, chopped
¼ teaspoon saffron threads or ½ teaspoon turmeric
1 cinnamon stick broken in two
1 cup apricot nectar
½ cup dry white wine
salt and freshly ground black pepper
½ cup pitted prunes, soaked
1 cup dried apricots, soaked
1 tablespoon honey
3 teaspoons lemon juice
1 tablespoon toasted sesame seeds

Chicken gado

SERVES 4

17½oz (500g) chicken
  tenderloins
1½ cups medium-grain rice
7oz (200g) green beans,
  trimmed and halved
2oz (60g) roasted unsalted
  peanuts
SATAY MARINADE
½ cup peanut butter
½ teaspoon chilli powder
½ teaspoon ground ginger
2 tablespoons lemon juice
1 tablespoon brown sugar
½ cup coconut milk

1. Place all marinade ingredients in a pan, heat and stir to combine. Place tenderloins in a non-metallic dish and stir in enough marinade to coat well. Cover and marinate at least 30 minutes in refrigerator.

2. Cook rice in boiling, salted water until tender, about 15 minutes. Drain well. Steam beans until tender but still crisp, then drain. Mix rice, beans and half the roasted peanuts together. Keep hot.

3. Heat the barbecue grill and add the tenderloins. Cook for 2 minutes on each side on high heat, brushing with marinade during cooking. Heat extra marinade on side of barbecue.

4. Pile rice into centre of heated plates. Arrange 2 or 3 tenderloins over the rice, top with heated marinade and sprinkle with remaining roasted peanuts.

Chicken jambalaya

SERVES 6

3lb 5oz (1½kg) chicken pieces
2 tablespoons oil
2 onions, chopped
1 clove garlic, chopped
1 green bell pepper (capsicum),
　chopped
1 celery stalk, chopped
1 cup medium-grain rice
1 cup drained chopped canned
　tomatoes
2 cups chicken stock
1 bay leaf
pinch of chilli powder
½ teaspoon dried thyme
salt and freshly ground black
　pepper
1 cup chopped sausage such as
　salami
¼ cup parsley, chopped

1. Heat oil and fry chicken pieces until golden. Remove from pan and reserve. Add onions, garlic, bell pepper and celery and fry over moderate heat until onions are tender. Add rice and toss over heat for about 2 minutes. Add tomatoes and replace reserved chicken in pan. Add stock with bay leaf, chilli powder, thyme, salt and pepper.
2. Bring to boil, cover and reduce heat to simmer. Cook until chicken is tender and liquid is absorbed. Preheat oven to 350°F (180°C). Transfer chicken mixture to shallow ovenproof dish, add sausage and cook in for 10 minutes. Serve garnished with chopped parsley.

Morgh polo

SERVES 4

1. Cover the rice with water, add the salt and soak for 2 hours. Drain thoroughly. Set aside.

2. Cut each thigh fillet into 3 or 4 pieces. Heat two-thirds of the butter in a large, heavy-based saucepan and brown the chicken well on all sides over high heat. Remove to a plate.

3. Add remaining butter and sauté the onion and pine nuts. Add thyme, salt, pepper and cinnamon. Add the drained rice and stir to coat well.

4. Heat chicken stock to boiling and pour over the rice. Return chicken pieces to saucepan and stir in apricots and raisins. Bring back to the boil for 2 minutes, then lower the heat, cover the saucepan and simmer for 10 minutes.

5. Place a folded tea towel under the saucepan lid, pressing lid down tightly. Turn heat down to very low and cook for 30–35 minutes undisturbed. Fluff rice with a fork and serve hot.

1 cup long-grain rice
1 teaspoon salt
28oz (800g) chicken thigh
    fillets
2oz (60g) butter
1 onion, finely chopped
¼ cup pine nuts
1 sprig thyme, leaves removed
    and stalk discarded
salt and freshly ground black
    pepper
¼ teaspoon ground cinnamon
2½ cups chicken stock
½ cup dried apricots, diced
½ cup raisins

Chicken with vegetables & rice

SERVES 4

1. Place rice, stock, soy sauce and 1 tablespoon sake or sherry in a saucepan and bring to the boil over a medium heat. Reduce heat to simmering, cover and simmer for 15 minutes. Remove pan from heat and stand, covered, for 5 minutes.

2. Heat oil in a wok or frying pan over a medium heat, add chicken and stir-fry for 3–4 minutes or until chicken is cooked.

3. Add mushrooms, tofu, carrots and leek and stir-fry for 2 minutes or until vegetables are just tender. Stir in remaining sake or sherry.

4. Add chicken mixture to rice, toss to combine and heat over a low heat for 4–5 minutes or until any excess moisture evaporates. Serve immediately garnished with parsley.

2 cups short-grain rice, rinsed and well drained
4 cups chicken stock
1 tablespoon soy sauce
¼ cup sake or dry sherry
2 tablespoons vegetable oil
2 boneless chicken breast fillets, sliced
4oz (125g) button mushrooms, sliced
2oz (60g) tofu, sliced
2 carrots, cut into thin strips
1 leek, sliced
¼ bunch parsley, chopped

Coconut fried chicken

SERVES 4

2lb 4oz (1kg) chicken pieces
1 cup coconut milk
1 onion, chopped
2 cloves garlic, crushed
¼ cup fresh cilantro
    (coriander), chopped
1 tablespoon desiccated
    coconut
1 large fresh red chilli, chopped
½in (12mm) piece fresh ginger,
    finely grated
2 teaspoons ground turmeric
1 teaspoon ground cumin
1 teaspoon brown sugar
2 tablespoons lemon juice
zest of ½ lemon, finely grated
1 cup brown rice, cooked and
    kept warm
½ cup wild rice, cooked and
    kept warm

1.   Place chicken, coconut milk, onion, garlic, cilantro, coconut, chilli, ginger, turmeric, cumin, sugar, lemon juice and lemon zest in a saucepan and bring to the boil over a medium heat. Reduce heat to simmering and simmer for 20 minutes or until chicken is just cooked and sauce is very thick.

2.   Remove chicken from pan and drain. Reserve sauce and keep warm. Place chicken under a preheated hot grill and cook for 3–5 minutes each side or until golden and crisp. Combine brown rice and wild rice. Serve chicken on a bed of rice topped with reserved sauce.

Chicken rice loaf

SERVES 8

4 cups finely chopped cooked
   chicken
2 cups cooked medium-grain
   rice
1 cup soft breadcrumbs
½ cup chopped onion
⅓ cup chopped pimientos
¼ cup fresh parsley, chopped
½ teaspoon salt
¼ teaspoon freshly ground
   black pepper
2 cups chicken stock
3 eggs, beaten

1. Preheat oven to 350°F (180°C).
Combine chicken, rice, bread crumbs,
onion, pimientos, parsley, salt, pepper, 2
cups of stock and eggs in a large bowl and
mix well.

2. Arrange extra pimiento strips in bottom
of greased loaf tin. Add chicken mixture and
pack firmly into tin.

3. Bake for 40 minutes. Allow to cool for
10 minutes before removing from tin. Serve
with a salad and tomato chutney.

Turkey rice

1. Combine the rice with 3¾ cups water in a saucepan. Bring to the boil, reduce heat to low, cover and cook for 15 minutes. Remove pan from heat, allow to stand covered for 10 minutes.

2. In a heavy-based frying pan combine onion, garlic, seasonings and turkey and brown. Break-up the meat to prevent large lumps forming, continue stirring to keep a good consistency.

3. Once it is almost brown add chickpeas and let meat continue to brown.

4. When meat is ready drain any remaining fat from the frying pan, add rice and stir until well blended.

2½ cups cooked rice
½ onion, diced
3 cloves garlic
salt and freshly ground black
   pepper
¾ teaspoon allspice
½ teaspoon ground cinnamon
1 teaspoon garlic powder
9oz (250g) minced turkey
   breast
15oz (450g) can chickpeas

Indian chicken with yellow rice

SERVES 4

1. Fry chicken until golden. Cut into bite-sized pieces. Heat butter and fry onions and garlic until tender. Blend in curry powder, ginger and cinnamon, cook, stirring, for 1 minute.

2. Add zest, juice, stock and lemon juice with orange segments and sultanas. Dissolve cornflour in a little water and add, stir until it boils and thickens. Season with salt and pepper. Add chicken and simmer on low heat for about 5 minutes.

3. To make the spiced yellow rice, combine rice, stock and spices in a saucepan. Bring to the boil, reduce heat to low, cover and cook for 15 minutes. Season and remove pan from heat. Allow to stand covered for 10 minutes. Gently fork butter through rice before serving.

4. Serve the chicken with spiced yellow rice and toasted almonds.

24oz (750g) chicken wings or pieces
½oz (15g) butter
2 onions, thinly sliced
1 clove garlic, crushed
3 teaspoons curry powder
1 teaspoon ground ginger
½ teaspoon ground cinnamon
grated zest and juice of
  1 orange
2 cups chicken stock
2 teaspoons lemon juice
2 cups fresh orange segments
½ cup sultanas
3 teaspoons cornflour
salt and freshly ground black
  pepper
½ cup toasted almonds
SPICED YELLOW RICE
2 cups medium-grain rice
4 cups chicken stock
4 cloves
1 bay leaf
2in (5cm) stick cinnamon
2 cardamom pods
½ teaspoon turmeric
salt and freshly ground black
  pepper
½oz (15g) butter

Broccoli chicken & rice

SERVES 4

10½oz (300g) can condensed
   cream of broccoli soup
¾ cup rice
1 cup broccoli florets
½ teaspoon paprika
½ teaspoon salt
½ teaspoon pepper
4 skinless chicken breast fillets
3oz (90g) aged Cheddar, grated

1. Preheat oven to 380°F (190°C). Mix soup, rice, broccoli, paprika, salt and pepper in a two litre baking dish with 1 cup water.

2. Place chicken on top of rice mixture and sprinkle with paprika, salt and pepper and top with cheese.

3. Cover with aluminium and bake for 40 minutes.

4. Remove foil and bake for another 5–10 minutes until chicken and rice is cooked.

Malaysian chicken curry & nut rice

SERVES 4

3lb 5oz (1½kg) chicken breasts
  and wings
½oz (15g) butter
1 tablespoon oil
1 tablespoon curry powder
3 onions, sliced
1 clove garlic, crushed
2 tomatoes, peeled and
  chopped
15oz (450g) canned pineapple
  pieces, drained, liquid
  reserved
1 cup chicken stock
salt and freshly ground black
  pepper
½ cup coconut milk
1 Lebanese cucumber, diced
NUT RICE
1oz (30g) butter
6 cups cooked medium-grain
  rice
½ cup pecans or chopped
  almonds
salt and freshly ground black
  pepper

1. Cut chicken into bite-size pieces. Heat butter and oil, brown chicken, remove, then add curry powder, onions and garlic. Cook, stirring, for 2 minutes. Add tomatoes, pineapple liquid and chicken stock. Season with salt and pepper. Add coconut milk, replace chicken and simmer until tender, about 25 minutes. Add pineapple pieces and cucumber, simmer until heated.
2. To make the nut rice, melt butter, add rice and nuts to pan and toss over moderate heat with fork until heated. Season with salt and pepper.
3. Serve the chicken spooned over the nut rice.

Risotto espanole

SERVES 4

1. Coat the chicken with paprika. Heat the olive oil in a large saucepan and sauté the garlic for 1 minute. Add the chicken pieces and cook until golden on both sides. Remove from the pan and cut into strips.

2. In the same pan, add the onion and cook until softened. Add the rice and stir well to coat. Add the wine and simmer until the liquid has been absorbed and the alcohol has evaporated.

3. Add ½ cup of hot stock, the chicken strips, taco sauce, tomato paste, tomatoes, orange juice and zest and bell pepper and stir thoroughly to combine. When all the liquid has been absorbed, add another half-cup of hot stock into rice mixture and cook, stirring constantly, until liquid is absorbed. Continue cooking in this way until all the stock is used and the rice is tender.

4. Serve in individual bowls, garnished with sour cream, parsley and extra orange zest.

2 skinless chicken breast fillets
1 teaspoon paprika
1 tablespoon olive oil
2 cloves garlic, finely chopped
1 onion, finely chopped
2 cups Arborio rice
½ cup red wine
3 cups chicken stock, heated
¾ cup taco sauce
2 tablespoons tomato paste
2 large tomatoes, chopped
juice and zest of 1 orange
1 green bell pepper (capsicum), sliced
½ cup sour cream
½ cup parsley, chopped

Peking duck risotto

SERVES 4

1. If the Peking duck is whole, cut into manageable portions. Strip all the flesh from the bones, and reserve skin. Slice the meat and set aside until required.

2. In a saucepan, heat the olive oil and sesame oil and add the scallions. Cook gently for 2 minutes until softened, then add the rice and stir to coat. Add the wine and allow the liquid to absorb while stirring. Add 1 cup hot stock and the bok choy to rice mixture and cook, stirring constantly, until liquid is absorbed. Add another cup of stock and the duck meat and cook, stirring until the liquid is absorbed.

3. Add the final cup of stock and the water chestnuts and stir. When all the liquid has been absorbed, remove the pan from the heat. Add the fresh herbs and mix well. Serve the risotto garnished with crispy duck skin.

1 cooked Peking duck
1 tablespoon olive oil
1 tablespoon toasted
   sesame oil
8 scallions (spring onions),
   finely chopped
2 cups Arborio rice
1 cup dry white wine
3 cups rich duck stock, heated
4 baby bok choy, halved or
   quartered lengthwise
7oz (200g) sliced water
   chestnuts, drained
½ cup fresh cilantro
   (coriander), chopped
½ cup fresh parsley, chopped

Speedy chicken & rice

SERVES 4

2 tablespoons olive oil

2lb 4oz (1kg) chicken wings

1⅔ cups tomato juice

1 packet French onion soup mix

3 teaspoons brown sugar

¼ teaspoon dried oregano

1 red bell pepper (capsicum), chopped

1 green bell pepper (capsicum), chopped

¼ cup parsley, chopped

1½ cups medium-grain rice

1. Heat oil in a frying pan and cook chicken wings until golden. Remove from pan and set aside.

2. Drain any juices from pan. Combine tomato juice, soup mix, brown sugar and oregano and add to the pan with the chicken wings. Cover and cook over medium heat for 20–25 minutes or until tender. During the last 5 minutes of cooking, add bell peppers.

3. Combine the rice with 2¼ cups water in a saucepan. Bring to the boil, reduce heat to low, cover and cook for 15 minutes. Remove pan from heat, allow to stand covered for 10 minutes. Grease individual moulds and spoon hot rice into moulds, press firmly, then turn out onto a serving plate. Garnish with parsley.

Stir-fried chicken & chilli

SERVES 4

3 tablespoons vegetable oil
1 onion, sliced
2 cloves garlic, crushed
¼ cup fresh cilantro (coriander) leaves and root, chopped
1 large fresh red chilli, chopped
4 boneless chicken breast fillets, sliced
4oz (125g) button mushrooms, sliced
2 cups basmati or jasmine rice
4 cups chicken stock
4 scallions (spring onions), chopped
1 small cucumber, sliced
1 tablespoon Thai fish sauce

1. Heat oil in a saucepan over a medium heat, add onion, garlic, cilantro and chilli and stir-fry for 2–3 minutes or until onion is golden and tender.

2. Add chicken to onion mixture and stir-fry for 2–3 minutes or until chicken is brown and cooked. Stir in mushrooms and cook for 1 minute longer. Remove chicken mixture from pan and set aside.

3. Stir rice into the same saucepan and cook over a medium heat, stirring, for 2 minutes. Pour stock into pan and bring to the boil. Reduce heat to simmering, cover and simmer for 15 minutes. Remove pan from heat and stand, covered, for 5 minutes.

4. Add chicken mixture, scallions, cucumber and fish sauce to rice and toss to combine. Return pan to a low heat and cook, stirring occasionally, for 3–4 minutes or until mixture is heated through.

Sultana orange chicken

SERVES 4

1. Combine lemon juice, onion, orange zest, salt, pepper and cinnamon and pour over chicken. Marinate in refrigerator for 1–2 hours, turning several times. Remove from marinade and pat dry.

2. Preheat oven to 350°F (180°C). Heat 3 tablespoons ghee in a pan and brown chicken lightly. Brush a baking dish with remaining ghee, then add drumsticks. Brush with marmalade then sprinkle with crushed peppercorns and mint. Bake for 45 minutes or until cooked, basting occasionally with ghee.

3. To make the orange sultana rice, combine rice with chicken stock, orange juice and zest. Bring to the boil, reduce heat to low, cover and cook for 15 minutes. Remove pan from the heat and allow to stand for 10 minutes. Stir through sultanas and almonds. Sprinkle with orange zest.

4. To make the curried sultanas, heat oil, add curry powder and cook 1 minute. Add almonds and toss over moderate heat for 2 minutes. Add sultanas and stir until plump.

5. Serve chicken with orange sultana rice and curried sultanas.

8 chicken drumsticks
½ cup lemon juice
1 small onion, finely chopped
zest of 1 large orange
1 teaspoon salt
freshly ground black pepper
½ teaspoon ground cinnamon
2½oz (75g) ghee or butter
2–3 tablespoons sieved orange
   or apricot marmalade
2 tablespoons coarsely crushed
   peppercorns
1 tablespoon dried mint
ORANGE SULTANA RICE
1 cup medium-grain brown rice
1½ cups chicken stock
½ cup orange juice
grated zest of 1 orange
2–3 cups sultanas
¼ cup flaked or slivered toasted
   almonds
thin strips of orange zest
CURRIED SULTANAS
3 tablespoons oil
1 teaspoon curry powder
¼ cup whole blanched almonds
1 cup sultanas

Spanish chicken & rice

SERVES 6-8

1. Cut the chicken in serving-size pieces, wash and sprinkle with salt. Brown chicken over medium heat in a large heavy-based frying pan until golden.

2. Heat oil in a large saucepan at medium heat. Stir in crumbled bacon and ham. Brown for 3 minutes, stirring often. Remove with slotted spoon, and set aside.

3. Stir in onion, garlic and red bell pepper. Stir over medium heat until onion softens, about 3–5 minutes.

4. Add chopped tomato, green bell pepper, olives, capers, oregano and tomato sauce. Stir for 2 minutes.

5. Add 1 cup of water and reserved chicken. Cook for 15 minutes over medium heat, turning occasionally.

6. Raise heat to high and add 3 more cups water. Bring to the boil and add rice, mix well. Bring to the boil again. Lower heat to medium and allow to cook uncovered until water is absorbed. Taste for seasoning and add salt if necessary.

7. Lower heat, cover and cook for 20 minutes. To serve, top with asparagus and baby peas.

3lb 5oz (1½kg) whole chicken
2 teaspoons salt
4 tablespoons olive oil
1oz (30g) cooked bacon, crumbled
2oz (60g) cooked ham, chopped
1 medium onion, chopped
2 cloves garlic, minced
1 red bell pepper (capsicum), deseeded and chopped
2 medium tomatoes, chopped
1 green bell pepper (capsicum), deseeded and chopped
½ cup pimento stuffed green olives
1 tablespoon capers, chopped
1 teaspoon dried oregano
1½ cups tomato sauce
2 cups white rice
4oz (125g) cooked asparagus, cut in pieces
1 cup cooked baby peas

Turmeric chicken with rice

SERVES 4

2oz (60g) tamarind pulp
2 tablespoons olive oil
4 onions, thinly sliced
8 chicken skinless thigh pieces
2 tablespoons ground turmeric
1in (25mm) piece fresh ginger,
    thinly sliced
2 tablespoons sugar
2 teaspoons salt
4–6 fresh red chillies, chopped
SPICED BROCCOLI RICE
1 head broccoli, cut into florets
1 tablespoon vegetable oil
1 clove garlic, crushed
1 teaspoon cumin seeds
1 teaspoon ground cumin
½ teaspoon ground coriander
½ teaspoon cayenne pepper
2 cups long-grain rice
4 cups chicken stock

1. Place tamarind in a bowl, cover with hot water, let stand until pulpy, then strain. Reserve liquid and discard pulp.

2. Heat olive oil in a frying pan over a medium heat. Add onions and cook for 3–4 minutes or until onions are golden. Remove onions from pan and set aside.

3. Dust chicken with turmeric, add to same pan and cook for 5 minutes each side. Add 2 cups water, tamarind liquid, onions, ginger, sugar, salt and chillies to pan and bring to the boil. Reduce heat to simmering, cover and simmer for 25–30 minutes.

4. To make spiced rice, steam broccoli until it just changes colour. Drain, rinse under cold running water and set aside. Heat oil in a saucepan, add garlic, cumin seeds, ground cumin, cilantro and cayenne pepper and cook, stirring, for 1 minute or until fragrant. Stir in rice and cook for 1 minute longer.

5. Stir chicken stock into rice mixture and bring to the boil. Reduce heat to simmering, cover and simmer for 15 minutes. Remove pan from heat and stand, covered, for 5 minutes. Serve with chicken.

Chinese chicken rice & peanuts

SERVES 4

1 tablespoon peanut oil
17½oz (500g) chicken
    tenderloins
2 scallions (spring onions),
    finely sliced
8 flat brown mushrooms, sliced
2 cups cooked long-grain rice
¼ cup parsley, chopped
¼ cup roasted peanuts
PEANUT DRESSING
½in (12mm) piece fresh ginger,
    grated
¼ cup crunchy peanut butter
2 tablespoons soy sauce
1 tablespoon sesame oil
2 tablespoons lemon juice

1. Heat oil in a wok and stir-fry chicken and scallions for 5 minutes or until chicken is cooked, then add mushrooms and stir-fry for 1 minute.

2. Make dressing by mixing ginger, peanut butter, soy sauce, sesame oil and lemon juice together.

3. Add cooked rice and toss dressing through. Continue to stir-fry until rice is hot.

4. Serve garnished with chopped parsley and peanuts.

dessert

Granny apple rice pancakes

SERVES 4

1. Combine all the ingredients.
2. Mix well to create a batter.
3. Cook 1 dessertspoon of the mixture in butter or oil for approximately 1½ minutes each side or until golden.

9oz (250g) cooked long grain rice
1 grated Granny Smith apple
½ cup honey
1 egg
½ cup self-raising flour
¾ cup milk
butter or oil for frying

Caramel banana rice

SERVES 4

1. Melt butter over medium heat then add sugar and sliced bananas.
2. Stir gently and add cream and rice.
3. Simmer for 2 minutes.

1oz (30g) butter
½oz (15g) brown suggar
3 sliced bananas
½ cup thin cream
4oz (125g) cooked wholegrain rice

Fruity rice delight

SERVES 2

2½ cups low-fat milk
1 cup long grain white rice
½ teaspoon vanilla extract
½ cup sugar
6 fresh dates, chopped
2 tablespoons cream
cinnamon sugar for sprinkling

1. Combine milk, rice, vanilla extract and sugar in a saucepan.

2. Bring to the boil over medium heat, then reduce to a simmer and cook for 20 minutes. Stir often to prevent the rice mixture from sticking.

3. Chop 6 fresh dates into small pieces and stir through the rice mixture, then stir through 2 tablespoons of cream.

4. Sprinkle with cinnamon sugar.

Mandarins in an almond lake

SERVES 4

2½ cups milk
½ cup sugar
1 teaspoon almond essence
⅓ cup ground rice
11oz (315g) can mandarin
  segments
¼ cup flake almonds

1. In a saucepan, combine milk, sugar, almond essence and rice. Stirring continuously and bring to the boil. Simmer, still stirring, for 5 minutes. Transfer to a bowl, cover and cool completely.

2. Drain mandarins. Spoon rice into individual dishes. Arrange mandarins on top and sprinkle with almond flakes.

Coconut rice

SERVES 4-6

1. Place all ingredients in a slow cooker and stir with a wooden spoon until combined.
2. Cook on a low setting for 8 hours.
3. Serve with stewed fruit or fruit compote.

21fl oz (600ml) milk
21fl oz (600ml) coconut milk
4oz (125g) arborio rice
2oz (60g) palm sugar, grated

Fruit salad rice

SERVES 4

2½ cups orange juice
3 cups cooked medium-grain
   rice
2 tablespoons honey
1 cup whipped cream
2 peaches, diced
1 cup diced honeydew melon
1 cup diced rockmelon
1 punnet strawberries, hulled
   and halved
3 passionfruit

1. Heat orange juice, add rice, bring to the boil, then lower heat to a simmer. Stir occasionally until almost all juice is absorbed. Remove from heat, add honey, allow to cool.

2. Fold whipped cream through rice. Combine kiwifruit, honeydew, pawpaw and strawberries, spoon fruits into a ring over rice. Spoon over passionfruit pulp.

3. Serve with extra whipped cream.

Index

Published in 2013 by
New Holland Publishers
London • Sydney • Cape Town • Auckland
www.newhollandpublishers.com

Garfield House 86–88 Edgware Road London W2 2EA United Kingdom
1/66 Gibbes Street Chatswood NSW 2067 Australia
Wembley Square First Floor Solan Road Gardens Cape Town 8001 South Africa
218 Lake Road Northcote Auckland New Zealand

A catalogue record of this book is available at the British Library and the National Library of Australia.

ISBN: 9781742573786

Managing Director: Fiona Schultz
Design: Lorena Susak
Proofreader: Jodi De Vantier
Production Director: Olga Dementiev
Printer: Toppan Leefung Printing Limited (China)

10 9 8 7 6 5 4 3 2 1

Texture: Shutterstock photo

Follow New Holland Publishers on
Facebook: www.facebook.com/NewHollandPublishers

UK £9.99
US $14.99